COVENANT • BIBLE • STUDIES

Miracles of Jesus

James L. Benedict

faithQuest® ♦ Brethren Press®

Miracles of Jesus
Covenant Bible Studies Series

© 2011 *faithQuest*®. Published by Brethren Press®, 1451 Dundee Avenue, Elgin, IL 60120. For publishing information, visit www.brethrenpress.com.

Cover photo © 2011 Wendy McFadden. Used by permission.

Library of Congress Cataloging-in-Publication Data

Benedict, James L. (James Lloyd), 1959-
  Miracles of Jesus / James L. Benedict.
     p. cm. — (Covenant Bible studies series)
  Includes bibliographical references.
  ISBN 978-0-87178-171-0
  1. Jesus Christ—Miracles—Study and teaching. I. Title.

  BT366.3.B46 2011
  232.9'55--dc23
                           2011035452

15 14 13 12 11   1 2 3 4 5

Manufactured in the United States of America

Contents

Foreword

The Covenant Bible Studies series provides *relational* Bible studies for people who want to study the Bible in small groups rather than alone.

Relational Bible study is marked by certain characteristics that differ from other types of Bible study. We are reminded that relational Bible study is anchored in covenantal history. God covenanted with people in Old Testament history, established a new covenant in Jesus Christ, and covenants with the church today. Thus, this Bible study is intended for small groups of people who can meet face-to-face on a regular basis and share frankly and covenant with one another in an intimate group.

Relational Bible study takes seriously a corporate faith. As each person contributes to study, prayer, and work, the group becomes the real body of Christ. Each one's contribution is needed and important. "For just as the body in one and has many members, and all the members of the body, though many, are one body, so it is with Christ. . . . Now you are the body of Christ and individually members of it" (1 Cor. 12:12, 27).

Relational Bible study helps both individuals and the group claim the promise of the Spirit and the working of the Spirit. As one person testified, "In our commitment to one another and in our sharing, something happened. . . . We were woven together in love by the Master Weaver. It is something that can happen only when two or three or seven are gathered in God's name, and we know the promise of God's presence in our lives."

In a small group environment, members aid one another in seeking to become

- biblically informed so they better understand the revelation of God;
- globally aware so they know themselves to be better connected with all of God's world;

- relationally sensitive to God, self, and others.

For people who choose to use this study in a small group, the following intentions will help create an atmosphere in which support will grow and faith will deepen.

1. As a small group of learners, we gather around God's word to discern its meaning for today.
2. The words, stories, and admonitions we find in scripture come alive for today, challenging and renewing us.
3. All people are learners and all are leaders.
4. Each person will contribute to the study, sharing the meaning found in the scripture and helping bring meaning to others.
5. We recognize each other's vulnerability as we share out of our own experience, and in sharing we learn to trust others and to be trustworthy.

The questions in the "Suggestions for Sharing and Prayer" section are intended for use in the hour preceding the Bible study to foster intimacy in the covenant group and to relate personal sharing to the Bible study topic, preparing one another to go out again in all directions to be in the world.

Welcome to this study. As you search the scriptures, may you also search yourself. May God's voice and guidance and the love and encouragement of brothers and sisters in Christ challenge you to live more fully the abundant life God promises.

Preface

Mention miracles these days and you are likely to provoke a debate. Some will insist that miracles are impossible, and that ancient stories about miracles simply reflect the ignorance, gullibility, and vivid imagination of people who lived in a pre-scientific era. Others will insist with equal conviction that miracles can, do, and have happened, and that modern skepticism reflects an arrogant intellectual prejudice against other ways of understanding what happens in the world around us.

If you have picked up this book hoping that it will settle this debate, you are certain to be disappointed. This is not a book for those who are primarily interested in broad, abstract, philosophical questions. This is a book for the church, and it is a book about the Bible. The church is the community of people whose hearts have been captured by the grace of God as it has been revealed in Jesus. For the church, the Bible is not a book about abstract philosophy. For the church, the Bible is a guide to faith and practice. The Bible helps those of us in the church to understand more clearly who God is, who we are, and how we are called to live. This book will approach the stories of Jesus' miracles with those concerns in mind.

Now, strictly speaking, the Bible tells us nothing about miracles. The word "miracle" never appears in the Scriptures. "Miracle" is a term derived from the Latin *miraculum*, which first meant an object of wonder, and later, as used by the church, came to mean a marvelous event caused by God. But no biblical author ever used the term *miraculum*. The biblical authors spoke instead of signs, wonders, and works of power. While those categories sometimes overlapped, each also tended to have a separate primary meaning. Each, however, involved some kind of event that was far from ordinary and which was thought to have its source in God.

All four of the Gospel authors are in agreement that such events were a big part of Jesus' ministry. Some contemporary Christians may be embarrassed by the miracles in the Gospels and elect instead to focus solely on the teachings of Jesus as found in the Sermon on the Mount or the parables. Yet in the Gospels, teachings and miracles appear side by side, and each is meant to help us understand the other. Without the stories of signs, wonders, and works of power, our understanding of Jesus is both diminished and distorted.

The purpose of this book is twofold. First, it is designed to guide groups through a serious examination of the role of miracles in the ministry of Jesus. Second, it is intended to promote discussion about how the signs, wonders, and works of power that Jesus performed help us understand better the One we call Lord and what it means to be his disciples.

James L. Benedict
Union Bridge, Maryland

1

The Unclean Woman
Mark 5:25-35

Personal Preparation

1. Recall a time in your life when you felt desperate. For what were you desperate? What were the circumstances that prevented you from being able to obtain what you wanted? How was the situation resolved? What role, if any, did your faith play in the resolution or in helping you cope?

2. In every social group, from kindergarten classes to society as a whole, there are always certain people who are pushed to the margins. Spend some time in prayer, remembering individuals or groups of people that others seem to go out of their way to avoid.

3. Read Leviticus 11–13 (three chapters) to get an idea of the range of things that could make one "ritually unclean" under the Law.

Suggestions for Sharing and Prayer

1. As you gather, make a special effort to greet each person in the group, to show an interest in anything they have to share about their lives, and to include them in the discussion. Do your best to make sure everyone feels especially welcome.

2. Certain groups are by their nature exclusive, while other groups may simply be so informally. Give some examples of both kinds of groups. Share memories of times you have felt excluded, avoided, or like an outsider

How did you handle the situation? Were you eventually
included or accepted? If so, how did that come about?
3. Many people these days are very worried about germs.
This concern fuels the sale of millions of dollars worth
of hand sanitizer and antibacterial soap. To what extent
do you share this widespread concern about germs and
contamination? If your congregation were to try to
restore the practice of using a common cup (one from
which all drink) in communion, would you support or
oppose the change? Why?
4. Purity is a major theme or emphasis in many religions,
though it may be defined in different ways. Jesus, in his
Sermon on the Mount, spoke of the "pure in heart"
(Matt. 5:8). The letter of James speaks of being "unstained by the world" (1:27). To what extent and in what
ways do you seek to be "pure" or "unstained"? Is being
"pure" or "unstained" important to you? Why, or why
not?
5. Close the time of sharing with a prayer. Be sure to join
hands. Begin with silence. After a minute or so, individuals may offer sentence prayers of confession, thanks-
giving, or petition. A leader should close the prayer when
it seems appropriate.

Understanding

Not so long ago, most people knew their neighbors and often considered them friends. They got together for picnics, loaned tools
to each other, and chatted over the backyard fence. Neighbors
were people you knew well and could count on if you ever needed them. But things have changed. While some folks might still
know their neighbors and socialize with them, most neighbors are
strangers who do little more than wave when they see each other.
Some don't even do that much.

Ever wonder when exactly people stopped talking to their
neighbors? The answer might surprise you—it was after the telephone was invented. Before the telephone, when you wanted to
talk to someone, proximity was important. Neighbors, being nearby, were top candidates. As a result, people built relationships

with their neighbors. But after the telephone came along, people could talk to whomever they wanted, even if that person lived across town or across the country. Telephones gave us the option of avoiding our neighbors and still being able to socialize.

Subsequent technological advances have only made the situation worse. Some people once thought that the Internet would facilitate interaction between people with different perspectives and values. What has actually happened is that the Internet has made it easier for most users to find like-minded folks, and participate in virtual communities where their views are more likely to be reinforced than challenged. In short, technology makes it easier for us to avoid people who are not like us.

Avoiding certain kinds of people is just something we humans do. When we are kids, our parents and other adults send us messages about which other kids they would prefer we spend our time with and which other kids they would rather we avoided. As we get older, our peers define who is "cool" and who isn't—and the social costs of hanging out with someone "uncool" can be steep. Even as adults we tend to cluster with folks like us in ethnicity, income, religion, and interests. And clustering with some often includes avoiding others.

To some degree, avoiding others is natural and often not particularly harmful. But when it gets serious—when we take great pains to avoid certain kinds of people, and when we start to justify it by claiming that those we avoid are evil or less than or dangerous or unworthy—then our avoidance becomes deeply problematic, especially from a spiritual point of view.

Our text deals with Jesus' encounter with a person many in that time and place would have taken great pains to avoid. The woman with a flow of blood belonged to one of several categories of people considered "unclean" and therefore to be avoided. Being "clean" or "unclean" in this sense had nothing to do with being physically dirty. Neither did it necessarily have anything to do with being physically sick. Some illnesses did make you unclean, but not all, while lots of things that had nothing to do with dirt or sickness could render you unclean. You could be well-washed and perfectly healthy, and still be unclean.

Being unclean simply meant that you were contaminated by something you did or something with which (or someone with whom) you came into contact. This contamination meant you were not fit to participate in certain religious acts. In order to become clean, certain other religious rituals were necessary, often along with a waiting period.

In the case of the woman in our story, she was unclean due to her flow of blood. This almost certainly refers to some kind of hemorrhage that caused her to effectively be constantly menstruating. According to the Law, a woman who was menstruating was by definition unclean. Thus, all women of childbearing age were unclean for a portion of the month. This woman, however, had suffered this way for twelve years. For twelve years, she had essentially been prohibited from participation in the rituals of Judaism. To make matters even worse, since contact with her by others would render *them* unclean, she was doomed by her disease to live in isolation. No wonder, then, that she had been willing to spend all she had on physicians, hoping for a cure.

But there was no cure from the physicians, so she continued to bleed. This means that, in the eyes of most, she had no business being in that crowd. She could get away with it because her form of being unclean could be hidden. But if the people around her had known her condition, many of them would have been disgusted and angry. How dare she expose everyone else to her uncleanness?

And, especially, how dare she reach out and touch the garment of a rabbi? A rabbi was by definition a religious person, who was expected to care about such things. When the woman touched the garment of Jesus, the garment became unclean. Because the garment touched Jesus, Jesus became unclean. At least that was how it was thought to work by many people at the time.

But that is not how it worked in our text. In this story from Mark's Gospel, the woman knows right away that she has been healed, and Jesus knows immediately that power has gone out from him. The result of contact was not contamination, but cure. Still, the woman must have been a little afraid when Jesus asked who had touched him. She may well have expected a rebuke from Jesus, if he became aware of the facts about her.

Yet she stepped forward, knelt in fear and trembling, and laid out the whole story. And Jesus responded with simple compassion: "Daughter, your faith has made you well; go in peace, and be healed of your disease" (v. 34). And then Jesus continued on to the house of a young girl who had died, where he restored her to life by taking her by the hand. Incidentally, touching a dead body as Jesus did was another action that normally made one unclean.

In both his teachings and his miracles, Jesus challenged the whole notion of what it was that made someone unclean, and what worrying about becoming unclean had to do with being religious. Jesus regularly and publicly ignored and violated all the rules about being clean or unclean, and he did it primarily to reach out to the many kinds of outcasts in his world. He refused to avoid the people he was supposed to avoid, and for that reason he lost a lot of potential supporters and even potential disciples.

One clear indication that we, as individuals and as a church, are following in Jesus' way is how we deal with the issue of including or avoiding. If we are too careful, and more concerned with purity than with practicing compassion, then we have forgotten our example. If we stay where we feel safe and wait for others to come to us rather than going out to where people are and addressing their needs, then we have strayed from the gospel way. And when we let our hearts be ruled by fear of the outcast, the outsider, the people who are not like us, then we lack faith in the power of God at work in us.

Discussion and Action

1. The introduction to the "Understanding" portion of the lesson suggests that the use of new technology may have some unanticipated and perhaps undesirable side effects. Consider how technology has affected your life. In what ways has it helped you connect with other people, including people with whom you otherwise might not have interacted? In what ways has it replaced day-to-day, face-to-face interaction with others? How well do you know your neighbors? What are some things we can

do to make sure technology doesn't isolate us from people who are different from us?

2. What kinds of people in modern times tend to be avoided, much like the woman with a flow of blood was avoided? Are we ever justified in avoiding certain kinds of people? Why, or why not? If anyone in the group has been someone whom others avoided, have that person (or persons) share the experience and what it felt like.

3. Make a list of animals that would be considered unclean according to the Law laid out in Leviticus and elsewhere in the Hebrew Bible. Look at the following texts to discover other sources of contamination: Leviticus 13:47-49; 15:1-6; 15:19-23; 21:10-12; Numbers 19:14-16. Discuss these laws and what purpose they may have served.

4. Jesus and his disciples were often charged with neglecting the purity laws. Why do you think Jesus took the approach he did to these rules? What role do you think his relative indifference to these laws made to the public perception of him? Be sure to consider various strata of the population (priests, Pharisees, scribes, merchants, laborers, the poor) as you answer this question.

5. Discuss ways in which your congregation is actively involved in reaching out to those on the margins of society, or those often excluded by other groups or individuals. In what ways might your congregation, or groups within it, reach out to include "the outcast"?

2

Blind Bartimaeus the Beggar
Mark 10:46-52

Personal Preparation

1. Gather a wider sense of the biblical perspective on begging and blindness by reading the following texts: [begging] Psalm 37:25; Psalm 109:6-10; Luke 16:20-22; Acts 3:2-5; [blindness] Exodus 4:11; Leviticus 19:14; Psalm 146:8; Isaiah 29:18; Matthew 11:5; Revelation 3:17.
2. When you encounter a beggar, how do you respond? Some beggars simply sit quietly with signs. Do you respond differently if the beggar speaks up? If so, how?
3. Make a list of the organizations in your community that help the destitute. Which, if any, of these organizations do you and/or your congregation support? What do you or your congregation do to help people in need?

Suggestions for Sharing and Prayer

1. Gather and greet one another. Then transition into a time of silence, reflecting on the people in need in your community and those who are directly involved in helping them. Try to picture them in your mind. Close the time of silence by reading Isaiah 58:6-9 in unison.
2. The prophet speaks of injustice, oppression, hunger, and homelessness. Name and discuss examples of these problems that you have encountered personally and others of which you are aware. When it comes to correcting these problems, which strategies seem to work and which don't?

3. Have group members share encounters they have had with strangers begging or asking for help. What concerns do you have when approached for help? Explore how such an encounter makes you feel, and what makes you more or less likely to respond positively to requests for help. For instance, does the age, gender, race, ethnicity, or personal appearance affect how likely you are to respond positively? What kind of feelings have you experienced when you have given beggars help and when you have passed by without giving help?

4. Share how you feel when you have to ask for help. Whom do you (or would you) ask? Have you ever had to ask a stranger for help? If so, what was that experience like?

5. With practice and tools (guide dogs, Braille, books on tape, etc.), the blind today can often live very productive lives, but this was seldom the case in biblical times. Imagine ways a person's life might change if he or she was to become blind. What activities that the sighted take for granted would be difficult or impossible if one were blind?

6. Enter a time of prayer together.

Understanding

Several years ago in an article on Puritan funeral practices published in a little-read academic journal, Laurel Thatcher Ulrich wrote, "Well-behaved women seldom make history." It was just an aside in the article, far from the main point. Professor Ulrich didn't give it much thought at the time, but soon she saw her phrase popping up in all sorts of unexpected places: newspaper articles, bumper stickers, T-shirts, coffee cups, etc. Realizing that her simple remark had taken on a life of its own, Ulrich decided to write a book by that title in which she described some of the women from history she had in mind when she came up with the phrase.

The well-behaved in general seldom make history, it seems. Folks who are overly concerned with keeping everyone else happy seldom do much to merit attention or to change the world we live in. Those who do—people like Martin Luther, Winston Churchill, Rosa Parks, or Dom Hélder Câmara—were often considered troublemakers in their own time. They knew that to get attention, sometimes you have to fuss, carry on, complain, and resist. In short, you might have to "misbehave" in order to make your voice heard, and you have to be willing to ignore those who try to "shush" you.

Bartimaeus, whom we meet in Mark 10, understood this, too. Bartimaeus was a blind man who had been reduced by his lack of sight to a life of begging. We encounter him sitting beside the road as Jesus and his disciples, accompanied by a large crowd, are leaving Jericho. Bartimaeus became aware that something was going on. Being blind, he couldn't see who or what it was that was drawing all the attention, but he evidently heard that it was Jesus. Also evidently, he had heard *about* Jesus. We don't know exactly what he had heard, but it was enough to make him a believer, and to make him want to get Jesus' attention.

So he began to cry out, "Jesus, Son of David, have mercy on me!" Some in the crowd did not take this well. Bartimaeus was a beggar, and beggars were supposed to sit quietly and beg humbly. If you have been in a big city lately, you may have seen how it goes. A beggar these days may have a sign, and may shake a cup with some coins in it to get your attention, but if beggars get more assertive than that, the police may be called. Beggars are supposed to remain low-key. But Bartimaeus was anything but low-key. He shouted; he wanted to be heard. When others told him to be quiet, he just shouted all the louder. He knew something important: well-behaved beggars may not get help. So he hollered.

Bartimaeus succeeded in getting Jesus' attention. But before we look at Jesus' response, let's reflect on the language Bartimaeus uses to get Jesus' attention. Bartimaeus shouts, "Jesus, Son of David, have mercy on me!" For Bartimaeus to call Jesus "Son of David" was to evoke a nostalgic longing, deep-seated in the Jewish soul, for an anointed king, a legitimate heir to the throne of the great King David. It was a declaration of faith, conviction, and confidence. It was also a statement charged with serious political implications.

These were dangerous words. Suggesting someone was the rightful Jewish king was considered sedition by the Roman authorities. Many people claiming to be liberators or leaders who would restore Israel to its glory days had already been hunted down and disposed of by the Roman troops. When Jesus is crucified later on, the claim "king of the Jews" is essentially the charge against him. It is what Pilate puts on the sign over Jesus' head as Jesus hangs there, suffering and dying. The sign is there to say, "This is what happens to people who try to pass themselves off as a king."

So it may be that this was what made some in the crowd object to Bartimaeus' shouts. Saying such things in public put Jesus and all his followers in danger. In trying to silence Bartimaeus, the crowd may have thought they were looking out for Jesus. Still, Bartimaeus would not be silenced. He was willing to run the risk of provoking the authorities in order to have a chance to be healed.

Jesus rewarded this willingness to take risks. He asked the others, "Call him here." And when Bartimaeus was finally before Jesus, Jesus asked him an interesting question: "What do you want me to do for you?" It is an interesting question because the answer seems so obvious: Bartimaeus must want his sight to be restored. But we see in this exchange something of Jesus' characteristic gentleness with victims and the vulnerable. Again and again in the healing miracles, it becomes clear that Jesus is interested in more than mere physical healing or restoration. Jesus is also interested in restoring dignity and empowering those who come for healing. He stops to ask, "What do you want me to do for you?" or "Do you want to be healed?" in order to show respect and give those in need a voice. In other cases, he gives those healed recognition as partners in the healing by saying, "Your faith has made you well."

When we think about how to interact with those who approach us for help, Jesus' example should come to mind. We must be careful to ask people what they want, rather than make assumptions or just tell them what we think they need. Like Jesus, we should have the goals of restoring their dignity and empowering them. This may take more time, thought, and effort than the "quick fix," but it is necessary if the "healing" is to be thorough and lasting.

Nearly all commentators have recognized that the story of Bartimaeus is highly and intentionally ironic. Bartimaeus was blind, yet he was one of the few who "saw" Jesus for who he really was, the Son of David, the promised messiah. So when Bartimaeus received his sight, he responded with more than simple gratitude. He took the bold step of becoming a disciple. We're told that he "followed [Jesus] on the way."

Well-behaved beggars know their place. The bold and brassy, on the other hand, refuse to be "shushed," refuse to be ignored, and refuse to believe that if people don't care God must not care either. The bold dare to believe that God cares, and that God will respond to their bold and passionate pleas.

Generally speaking, it was not the well-behaved who were drawn to discipleship. Rather, it was those bold enough to believe that Jesus was God's messenger and that through Jesus, God was revealing himself to the world in a new way. Those who became disciples used their boldness to go forth and proclaim the good news of Jesus: that sins could be forgiven, that everyone matters, and that there is a better way of life waiting for those who are bold enough to live it.

Discussion and Action

1. Many people consider religion, and especially Christianity, as an effective means for teaching people to be humble, quiet, and respectful. Discuss why people may think so, whether or not you agree, and why.

2. Where do you see a need for Christians to be less well-behaved or more outspoken? How might we who follow Jesus express ourselves more effectively? What methods and media might be used? If Christians were less well-behaved and more outspoken, do you think more or fewer people would be attracted to the church? Why? What other consequences might it have for the church?

3. When Bartimaeus referred to Jesus as "Son of David" it was a statement that could be heard as political. Later on, when early Christians proclaimed, "Jesus is Lord," it also carried political overtones, since a common Roman expression was "Caesar is Lord." What are some ways that being faithful followers of Jesus might bring Christians today into conflict with the powers that be?

4. Jesus rewards Bartimaeus for being outspoken and willing to take risks. Jesus' parable of the talents (see Matt. 25:14-30) may also be read as encouraging his followers to take risks. When was the last time faith led you, someone you know, or your congregation to take a risk? What happened? What are some risks you might take as an individual? What are some risks your congregation might take?

5. Discuss how Jesus interacted with Bartimaeus. Note that he asked Bartimaeus what he wanted. Especially when it comes to the discussion of poverty, many people who are not poor think they already know what the poor "really need." List some of the solutions to the problems of the poor that are offered by pundits. Then discuss whether these "solutions" can simply be imposed on the poor. If not, how might Jesus' strategy lead to better results?

3

Water into Wine
John 2:1-11

Personal Preparation

1. Take a look at some wedding magazines or websites (www.weddingchannel.com or www.brides.com are two possibilities). What is your impression of the kind of weddings these resources seem to promote? Reflect on your reaction to what you see.

2. Jesus carried out his ministry in a shame-and-honor culture. Think back to high school, which many experience as a kind of shame-and-honor culture. During adolescence, what others think of you matters a great deal. Think about your high school experience, including any moments when you were deeply embarrassed or shamed by a social blunder.

Suggestions for Sharing and Prayer

1. Greet one another and share joys and concerns. Share a gathering hymn, either by singing or by reading the lyrics of a verse or more in unison. Some possibilities include, "God is here among us," "Come, let us all unite to sing," "Here in this place," or "Holy Spirit, come with power."

2. Share memories of weddings you have attended, including how simple or extravagant they may have been. Discuss how you feel about all the time, money, and

emotion invested in many modern weddings. If you are married, how did you decide what style of wedding to have?

3. Have you ever witnessed something go wrong at a wedding or reception? If so, how did the bride and groom respond? How did others respond?

4. Share any experiences group members may have had of social blunders or deep embarrassment. What factors contributed to or created the embarrassment? How did others react? How long did the embarrassment or shame linger? What, if anything, helped the person to overcome or move on from the situation?

5. Enter into a time of prayer. Begin with a full minute of silence, during which each person should seek to quiet his or her thoughts. One way to do this is to focus on one's breathing: deliberately begin to breathe more slowly and more deeply. At the end of the minute, have someone guide the group in prayer with these statements: "Lord, be present"; "Lord, we are grateful"; "Lord, we are needful." After each statement, there should be a pause to allow members of the group to complete the prayer with short phrases like: "Lord be present in our midst" or "in [name a place]"; "Lord we are grateful for health" or "for peace," etc.; "Lord, we are needful of forgiveness" or "of wisdom," etc. Have the guide conclude the prayer with "Amen."

Understanding

Not so very long ago, weddings were often simple and inexpensive, especially for the lower and middle classes. Often, a bride and groom would simply make an appointment with their pastor, whom they might meet in the parsonage parlor, and have the wedding conducted then and there. Sometimes, the pastor's spouse and children were the only witnesses. In the last century, however, weddings among the middle class began to develop into much more elaborate and expensive events. In 2010, the average American wedding was said to cost between $15,000 and $25,000.

That, however, is a mere drop in the bucket compared to some weddings in the Arab world. It is not uncommon for parents in the Arab world to begin to save money for a daughter's wedding before the child is even born—or conceived! That is because a "proper" wedding involves 500 to 800 guests and the best food and entertainment that the parents can afford. Wedding budgets of $100,000 or more are hardly rare.

That probably sounds excessive to most of us, but in the culture of the Middle East putting on a proper wedding is incredibly important. It is one of the most critical points in life, and one's honor and reputation are on the line. Remember, shame and honor play a much bigger role in their culture than in ours. You may have heard news stories from the Middle East in which shame or loss of honor is the motive for murder or suicide. Shame and honor are that important, and weddings are a kind of make-or-break opportunity where honor is concerned.

Similar cultural values were at work at the wedding Jesus attended in John 2. There is really no way of knowing exactly why Jesus and his mother were invited. There is no reason to think it had to be the wedding of a close relative. It may have been a mere casual acquaintance, and yet not only Jesus and his mother were included, but also at least some of Jesus' disciples.

The similarity in cultural values also tells us something else important: running out of wine was a very, very bad thing. In terms of shame and honor, this was something shameful. It would mean the loss of much honor. Running out of wine was not just a problem; it was a potential disaster, a horrible humiliation. It is not clear how Mary became aware of this impending disaster, but when she did, she surely understood how serious it was. So she sought out Jesus and reported the problem. Jesus also surely grasped how serious it was, and yet his initial reaction was to decline the invitation to do something about it.

Several times in the New Testament Jesus refuses to do what others ask of him. At first, this simply seems to be another such instance. But in the end, it is an example of something much less common. It is an example of Jesus doing something he is at first reluctant to do.

What causes Jesus to change his mind? We aren't told exactly. What we are told is that his mother, Mary, tells on-looking servants: "Do whatever he tells you." This comes just *after* Jesus has said, "My hour has not yet come." In John's Gospel, Jesus is very clear about who he is and what he is supposed to be doing. He is the One sent by God to bring salvation and hope, the One who will inaugurate the new age—the age of the reign of God. Evidently, he has an idea of how he wants it all to unfold. That idea does *not* include kicking off his ministry by changing water into wine at some wedding in Cana! This isn't how or where or when he had imagined performing his first sign. He had other plans.

There is something appealing about the fact that Jesus had to change his plans. It fits John's description of Jesus as God incarnate—Jesus being God, but becoming one of us. The theologians talk about Jesus being fully human and fully divine. This is a great example of one of the ways Jesus was fully human. You can't be fully human and still be in total control. If you are human, you make plans and sometimes those plans get changed. That's what happened to Jesus at Cana of Galilee.

Eventually, Jesus concedes and saves the day. He prevents the disaster. He saves the honor of the couple and of the bride's family by turning water into wine. But he does more than that. He performs his first sign.

A sign—that's what John's Gospel calls the miracles he performs. In John's Gospel, the miracles are more than just supernatural good deeds. They are coded messages. For those who can interpret the signs, they provide important information. In this case, and in the case of all the signs that follow in the Gospel of John, the signs provide important information about who Jesus is, where Jesus has come from, and what his coming means for the world.

Part of the sign is how much wine Jesus produces—somewhere between 120 and 180 gallons, which is a lot more than would be needed at a wedding reception. Why so much? Abundant wine was a well-known symbol of the coming of the messianic age. Amos 9:13 reads: "The time is surely coming, says the LORD, when the one who plows shall overtake the one who reaps, and the treader of grapes the one who sows the seed; the mountains shall drip sweet wine, and all the hills shall flow with it." The prophet Joel also says the mountains will drip with sweet wine. These were understood to be texts about that time when God would enter history and begin to set things right. So abundance is part of the sign.

The One whom God promised to send has come—that is the information available to those who are able to interpret this, the first sign. And because Jesus is the One God promised to send, to join in the work that Jesus does is to become part of what God is doing in the world. That great opportunity is available for those who understand the signs.

But others miss the sign. All they see is a miracle, just another wonder worked by another wonder-worker. A miracle can lead to a kind of belief, but not the kind of belief Jesus is looking for. Near the end of the chapter we are told that when Jesus "was in Jerusalem during the Passover festival, many believed in his name because they saw the signs that he was doing" (John 2:23). But belief based on witnessing wonders, without understanding them as signs, is not authentic belief. That's why the next verses say: "But Jesus on his part would not entrust himself to them, because he knew all people and needed no one to testify about anyone; for he himself knew what was in everyone" (John 2:24-25).

In each of the Gospels, Jesus appears ambivalent about his own wonder-working power. He knows that the miracles he performs can be interpreted in multiple ways. He knows that miracles are as likely to mislead as to lead, to misinform as to reveal the truth. In John's Gospel, the signs are symbols; they point beyond themselves to deeper, more important realities. Genuine faith is not the inevitable result of witnessing wonders. It also requires a proper understanding of what one has witnessed. That proper understanding will be consistent with Jesus' teachings.

Discussion and Action

1. Most of Jesus' acts of power address what many of us would consider serious problems, like illness, demon

possession, hunger, or even death. By contrast, in this text, Jesus is confronted with a situation that could be described as simply a social blunder. Some might consider social embarrassment an unworthy target for Jesus' first exercise of his wonder-working power. Discuss whether you agree or disagree, and why.

2. The interaction between Jesus and his mother in this story is interesting. Mary seems to take it for granted that Jesus can and should do something. Jesus, however, is reluctant. Take a look at some other Gospel texts that describe Jesus' relationship with his family (for example, Matt. 12:46-50; Mark 3:21; John 7:1-9). Talk about ways in which being part of a flesh-and-blood family can complicate being a follower of Jesus.

3. The authors of the various Gospels can't seem to agree on the appropriate terminology to use in reference to Jesus' works of power. In Matthew's Gospel, for instance, Pharisees and teachers of the Law ask for a sign and Jesus declares that no sign shall be given "except the sign of the prophet Jonah" (Matt. 12:38-39). In John's Gospel, however, each work of power is called a sign. How might the two approaches be reconciled?

4. John's Gospel is critical of those who witness the signs but see only works of power. Indeed, Jesus himself seems ambivalent about his power to perform signs. If signs like those performed by Jesus were common today in the church, what effects might it have—positive or negative?

5. The turning of water into wine represents the fulfillment of promises that God will provide abundantly for all people. Consider ways in which individuals, groups, and congregations can participate in this work of providing abundance for those who have little or none.

4

Feeding a Crowd
Mark 6:30-44

Personal Preparation

1. Review some of the texts in scripture that speak of feeding the hungry. Here is a list with which to start: Psalm 146:6-8; Proverbs 25:21; Isaiah 58:6-8; Ezekiel 18:6-8; Matthew 25:31-36; Revelation 7:15-17. Reflect on each text, considering who in the text is hungry, who provides food, and what motivations are involved.
2. Hunger can refer to desire in general, not just for food. Spend time in self-examination, asking what it is that you most "hunger" for, and whether it is "food" that truly satisfies, or a craving for something else.

Suggestions for Sharing and Prayer

1. Gather and greet one another. Select a volunteer to lead a prayer after the time of sharing. Invite each member of the group who is willing to share any joys or concerns. When sharing is finished, the volunteer should pray, and after addressing the joys and concerns, say: "For this, Lord, we hunger and thirst." Participants may reply by naming something they desire for themselves or for others. After a participant names what they desire, the group replies in unison, "Lord, hear our prayer." When the volunteer leader senses that there will be no more sharing, he or she may close the prayer with "Amen."

2.   Share some of your favorite things to eat as leftovers, as
     well as things you don't like as leftovers. Is there any-
     thing that you consider even better as a leftover than it
     was the first time? Do you eat more, fewer, or about the
     same amount of leftovers as you did when you were
     growing up?
3.   If anyone in the group has ever worked in a restaurant,
     have them talk about how much food they saw wasted.
     If anyone in the group has ever worked or volunteered
     in a soup kitchen or other agency that feeds the poor
     and hungry, have them talk about their experiences.
4.   Share what you learned in your reflection on some of
     the texts that speak of feeding the hungry. How would
     you describe the themes you see in these verses?
5.   Share a memorable time that you have been fed, literal-
     ly or figuratively, by someone.
6.   Conclude the time of sharing and prayer by singing one
     of the following: "Guide me, O thou great Jehovah"
     (verse 1), "We plow the fields and scatter" (verse 1),
     "Let us break bread together," or "Grant us, Lord, the
     grace."

Understanding

I come from a family where leftovers were a regular part of the
cuisine. With five children to feed and sometimes undependable
employment, my parents couldn't afford to waste food. Leftover
meat from a dinner became lunchmeat for sandwiches the next
day. Extra boiled potatoes from dinner got sliced and fried for
breakfast. Even vegetables got reheated and eaten.

Most people, it seems, either love leftovers or loathe them.
Surveys suggest that the lovers are in the majority. One survey
indicated that 9 out of 10 Americans eat leftovers at least once
or twice a week, while 1 in 5 eats leftovers as many as five times
a week. Of course, nowadays, leftovers are at least as likely to
come from a restaurant as from a home-cooked meal. Fifty-two
percent of restaurant patrons take food home, and the contents of
all those doggy bags usually don't end up in a doggy dish.

It might surprise you to know how often the subject of leftovers comes up in the Bible. Several laws in Exodus concerning sacrifices include instructions for how leftovers are to be handled. In some cases, leftovers are to be burned. In others, leftovers belong to the priests. And in still others, leftovers belong to the person who brought the sacrifice in the first place. Also in Exodus, we learn of the prohibition against keeping leftovers of the daily gift of manna, except for the manna provided on the day before the sabbath.

Leftovers also show up in the story of Ruth, where Boaz invites Ruth to dine with him and then gives her the leftovers to take home to Naomi, her mother-in-law. Finally, Elisha performs a smaller version of the miracle credited to Jesus. Elisha feeds a hundred hungry men with a mere twenty loaves. These loaves were likely single servings, not like the loaves we buy today at the store or bake at home, so this was quite a feat. And, again, there were leftovers.

Mark's account of Jesus multiplying the loaves resembles but far surpasses the story of Elisha and the twenty loaves. With a mere five loaves and two fish, Jesus feeds not a hundred, but thousands. This story was very popular in the early church. We know that because it is one of very few stories that appear in all four Gospels. It also appears in some of the earliest Christian art. This was a story that resonated with people who lived in a time when food security was a problem, when malnutrition was common, and when a drought or war could and often did lead to starvation.

Though many found it meaningful, some did not grasp the meaning Jesus intended. In the Gospel of John we read of Jesus' reaction to a group that followed him around afterward, hoping he would do it again. Jesus said to them, "Very truly, I tell you, you are looking for me, not because you saw signs, but because you ate your fill of the loaves" (John 6:26). It is a good reminder that if you bring a selfish perspective to a reading of the Gospels, you are going to get them all wrong. If your approach is, "How can I get Jesus to give me what I want?" then you are starting off on the wrong foot.

The initiative in this story is not with people wanting bread, but with Jesus feeling compassion for people who are hungry. The text says he saw the great crowd and had compassion for them, for they were like sheep without a shepherd. The crowd that got fed had no idea when they came that Jesus was going to feed them. They had come just to see Jesus and perhaps to hear him teach.

Yet Jesus did feed them, and there were even leftovers—twelve baskets full. The detail about the leftovers stands out from a literary perspective. It seems unnecessary. Feeding the multitude is impressive enough without leftovers, and we are never told what becomes of these leftovers. So why mention them at all?

The leftovers are mentioned to remind us that our God is a more-than-enough God. Our God is not an almost-enough God, or a just-enough God. Our God is a more-than-enough God. As we have seen, that doesn't mean God will give us whatever we want whenever we want it. God may not even give us what we want when we think we *need* it. But God will give us what we really, truly need, and God will give us more than enough.

And, more than enough doesn't start with material things. It starts with peace, a sense of purpose, hope, and strength. Jesus, in his teaching, called people to stop striving and worrying so about things—even about clothes to wear and things to eat. God will provide, Jesus said. Rather than worry about that, Jesus said, seek first the kingdom of God and God's righteousness, and then all these things will be added unto you.

Jesus' message wasn't about how to get stuff, but about how and why to give your life to God. It was about why we were created, and how we can be redeemed, and what it means to be a disciple. It was aimed at changing people from persons who were looking for freebies into persons who were eager to give so that the needs of others might be met.

At the heart of that transformation was the realization that God is a more-than-enough God. Knowing this about God gives believers the confidence to stop worrying about themselves and to start working for the kingdom, to stop striving for that which can never satisfy and to start finding more contentment in loving and serving God than they ever thought possible.

All of us go through "not enough" periods now and then—times when our minds race and our hearts worry about where we are going to find resources to meet life's demands. But there are some people who seem to be "not enough" people all the time. I guess you might call them "never enough" people. They are never satisfied, always fearful, ever grasping. Some are rich and some are poor by the world's standards, but they are all poor spiritually, and no amount of money or property or possessions could ever make them feel like they had enough.

Jesus' message is good news for "not enough" people, which is all of us some of the time and some of us all of the time. The good news is that there is a cure for the "not enough" feeling—and the cure is *not* in getting more things. The cure is found in opening our hearts to the grace and power of God. God's grace and power help us see that our problem isn't that we do not have enough bread. Our problem is that we desire the wrong kind of bread. The grace and power of God in Jesus Christ point us toward the bread that satisfies—the bread from God's table—where we are always welcome . . . and where there is always more than enough.

Discussion and Action

1. As noted in the section above, the story of Jesus feeding the multitude appears in all four Gospels and was popular in the early church. Why do you think early Christians were especially taken by the story of this particular miracle? The story, while still well-known, seems to be somewhat less popular in the current age, particularly in affluent Western cultures. Why do you think this is true?

2. Just as Jesus was able to heal, but did not eliminate all illness, so Jesus was able to multiply the loaves but did not end all hunger. What might this suggest about the works of power Jesus did perform—especially about their purpose or meaning?

3. After multiplying loaves in John's Gospel, Jesus had trouble with some who followed him simply seeking more free bread. In what ways do people today choose to be involved with Jesus and/or the church for similar reasons? In what ways can churches get caught up in trying to attract crowds with "free bread"?

4. Talk about the "not enough" times in your spiritual journey. Then talk about times when you have been keenly aware of having God's more-than-enough blessing.

5. The lunch of five loaves and two fish reminds us that we also can contribute to God's work. While some might have scoffed at such a meager offering when the need was so great, Jesus received the gift and blessed it. Discuss times when you have been reluctant to share because you thought you couldn't offer enough to make a difference. Share any experiences you have had where you were surprised by how much was accomplished with few resources.

6. Share ways you can bring forth "loaves and fishes" for God to multiply. Think beyond the obvious—money and material things. Consider other resources you have, including time, skills you can teach or share, etc.

5

The Man by the Pool
John 5:1-18

Personal Preparation

1. Spend a day trying to be especially aware of moments
    when you feel impatient. What is going on when you
    feel that way? What, if anything, do you do to reduce
    your feeling of impatience? If you happen to be among
    others, observe them for signs of impatience as well.
    How do those who are impatient signal how they feel?
2. If possible, go to a body of water (pond, lake, river,
    ocean) and spend some time in meditation and prayer. If
    it is not possible to actually go, recall a time you spent
    near water, or imagine being there as you meditate and
    pray.

Suggestions for Sharing and Prayer

1. Place a large bowl of clean water on a stand or table
    around which the group can gather. As the group comes
    together, greet one another and take turns sharing exam-
    ples of ways that water can bring peace, joy, and even
    healing to people. Then use a few minutes of silence to
    breathe deeply and quiet your minds. Focusing on the
    surface of the water may help. Any who wish may touch
    the water.
2. Share about the day you spent paying special attention
    to the things that made you feel impatient. What sur-
    prised you most about yourself? About others? What
    signals do you give off when you are feeling impatient?

3. Discuss some of the challenges faced by people with chronic illnesses or a disability. Do not limit yourself to the physical challenges. Consider also the broader impacts of the condition—social, economic, emotional, and spiritual.

4. It has been said that "timing is everything." Wisdom is shown in waiting long enough, but not too long. Talk about a time in your life when you wish you had been more patient. What happened because you weren't? Then talk about a time in your life when you were too patient. What happened (or didn't happen) because you waited longer than you should have?

5. Name some activities you tend to put off when possible, and some that you seldom or never put off. Why do you think you are so eager to do some things, but not others?

6. Talk about how you handle sabbath observance. When and how do you observe sabbath? What activities do you generally avoid on your day of rest, and what activities do you typically engage in? What helps you engage more fully in sabbath rest? Do you wish you were stricter about observing a day of rest? Why, or why not?

Understanding

Our capacity for patience decreases as the speed of life increases. In 1900, it was considered amazing that you could send a letter from Miami to Seattle, and it would get there in only three weeks! In 1940, you could watch the news on newsreels only a week after it happened. In 1950, the letter that had taken three weeks to deliver half a century earlier now arrived in just one week. In 1990, overnight express mail came along. And since then, we instant message, video conference, etc.; communication takes place in "real" time.

So it is no surprise that patience is rare in today's world. We are used to getting what we want in moments, even microseconds. When I'm doing research, I find myself getting impatient when I have to wait five seconds for an article to download—an article I might otherwise have to travel several hours to get in person or wait days to receive through the mail. But instead of thinking about the hours or days it could have taken, all I think about is the second or two quicker it could have been transmitted.

Who among us couldn't benefit from learning to be more patient? And yet, we must ask, is patience *always* a virtue? In every situation? Regardless of what is at stake? The answer is clearly no. For proof, we need look no further than the story of Jesus' healing of the man who had been paralyzed for thirty-eight years.

This act of healing takes place in Jerusalem, near the Sheep Gate, where there was a pool with five porticoes, or covered porches. Because the pool had reputed healing properties, many sick people came to sit around the pool, filling the porticoes. It especially attracted people for whom other therapies had failed.

Lots of places throughout history have been known for their healing waters. In this case, the waters were said to have healing power for only the first person who entered the water after it had been stirred by a breeze. This might make more sense to us moderns if we remember that the word in Hebrew for spirit is the same as the word for breeze or wind. When the water stirred, it was believed that the Holy Spirit was active.

Of all the sick persons gathered there, Jesus approached one particular man, a man who had been paralyzed for thirty-eight years. Obviously, the likelihood that he could ever be first in the pool was slim. Nonetheless, he went to the place each day and waited. Jesus came up to the man and asked a curious question: "Do you want to be made well?" The man's reply is defensive. He explains why he hasn't been healed, implying that he is doing his best and noting that someone else always got to the water first. Jesus has compassion for the man's plight, and gives him the healing that he needed, along with orders to take up his mat and walk.

Up to this point, it is a rather unremarkable healing story. What makes it stand out is what follows. The newly healed man carrying his mat encounters some opponents of Jesus. These

opponents of Jesus take issue with the fact that the man is
carrying a mat on the sabbath. Work was prohibited on the sabbath, and carrying something around was considered work. So
they asked the man why he was doing this. After the man told the
story of his healing, the enemies of Jesus became angry that
Jesus was violating the sabbath and encouraging others to do so
as well.

Before we go further, it is necessary to say a couple of words
about terminology. You may have noticed that the enemies of
Jesus are referred to in the text as "the Jews." This is how John
always refers to Jesus' enemies. He has his reasons, which we
need not go into. What matters is that we stop and realize that
not all Jews were enemies of Jesus, then or since, and that what
John wrote does not justify anti-Semitism. Jesus was a Jew. All
his disciples were Jews. The man he healed in this case was a
Jew. There are no Gentiles in this story, so "the Jews" can only
mean *some* of the Jews, those with particular animosity toward
Jesus.

Jewish law permitted—even required—violation of the sabbath in order to save a life. But Jesus' act of healing here (and
also in Mark 2 and Luke 13) doesn't qualify as lifesaving. One
way to look at it is this: if a man has been paralyzed for thirty-
eight years, what is one more day? From the point of view of the
defenders of the sabbath, a loyal Jew ought to be willing to suffer at least one day in order to preserve something so central and
sacred as the sabbath tradition. Why, they wondered, couldn't
Jesus just be patient? After all, patience is a virtue.

Patience is a virtue, *sometimes*. Patience is a virtue when
patience is required, when events naturally unfold at their own
pace. Patience is a virtue when the outcome for which we are
waiting is beyond our control—when we can't make it happen.
But patience is not a virtue when others are suffering and we
have the ability to do something about it. Patience is not a virtue
when it makes our lives easier while making other peoples' lives
more difficult. For Jesus, a man who has been paralyzed for thirty-eight years *could* wait one more day to be healed, but he
shouldn't have to.

Jesus believed in the sabbath, but he believed differently than his opponents. As he put it, "The sabbath was made for humankind, and not humankind for the sabbath" (Mark 2:27). The sabbath was meant to be a day not just of rest but of restoration. So healing was not an act *against* the sabbath; it was an act in the very spirit of the sabbath.

The challenge for us, as we consider this story in our time, is to think about the opportunities we have that we are not seizing, to think about the things we know we should do but keep putting off. We all need rest, and sometimes we need time to reflect and sort out our thoughts. But deep down we know when we cross the line between patience and procrastination. We know when we are asking others to suffer, or to do without, or to do the work we should be doing, just because we don't want to do it . . . yet.

The story of healing in John 5 is there to remind us to be suspicious of our own motives, and to be careful about becoming complacent toward the suffering of others. It is always easy to come up with reasons—even "religious" reasons—to avoid doing things we don't want to do. It is especially tempting to try to justify suffering rather than relieve it—to say that those who suffer have brought it on themselves, that suffering builds character, or that it is just the way the world is. But as followers of Jesus we shouldn't be making excuses. We should be making a difference.

Discussion and Action

1. Take turns sharing ways that each of you has experienced an increase in the speed of life. What technologies have contributed to the increasing speed of modern life, and how? Do you think there is a natural or normal pace for humans? If so, do you think the current speed of life in the Western world is faster, slower, or just about the same as that natural or normal speed? Why?

2. At one time, so called "blue laws" prohibited a large variety of activities on Sunday. Much has changed in

most parts of the developed world, but some vestiges of the "blue laws" remain in many places. What kinds of limits have you encountered? What still can't be done on Sunday? Do you wish more or fewer activities were restricted? Why?

3. Jesus comes into conflict with some of the Jewish leaders when he refuses to refrain from performing healings on the sabbath. Do you find any merit in the argument that a man who had been ill thirty-eight years could certainly wait one more day? Why, or why not? What do you think of "slippery slope" arguments, which hold that small violations inevitably lead to major ones?

4. Think of history. Share some examples when people were asked to be patient, perhaps unjustly. Think of the present. What groups today are being asked to be patient? Would you see the story of Jesus healing on the sabbath as relevant for these groups and their situations? Why, or why not?

5. In the book of Job, the friends of Job who witness his suffering attempt to justify or explain it. How is this different from the way Jesus reacts when he encounters suffering? What can we do to be more like Jesus and less like Job's friends when we encounter suffering?

6

Good Friends
Luke 5:17-26

Personal Preparation

1. Make a short list (no more than six) of close friends you have had. Begin with early childhood and come up to the present. Think of the things you enjoyed doing with each friend and/or some of the special experiences you went through together. Spend time in prayer, thanking God for each of these friends and the ways in which they contributed to your development.

2. Read John 1:40-49. Note how both Andrew and Philip immediately introduce others to Jesus. Consider persons you might be able to introduce to Jesus, and how you could go about it.

Suggestions for Sharing and Prayer

1. As you gather and greet one another, remember to thank everyone present for their friendship and support. Once you are settled, take turns sharing about the person or persons who introduced you to Jesus or first brought you to church. Include when and how it took place, and whether you are still in touch with these people. When everyone has shared, have a volunteer pray a prayer of thanks for these people who have made such a difference in your lives.

2. Discuss what qualities you look for in a friend. As a group, make a list, and then rank the qualities in the list.

Where do you think you would be most likely to find people with these qualities? Where would you be least likely to find such people?

3. Some of us are extroverts and some of us are introverts. According to one definition, an extrovert is someone who gains energy from being with people, while an introvert is someone who spends energy being with people. Share how you would classify yourself, and why. Then talk about extroverts and introverts as friends. Is one or the other better at making or keeping friends? Why, or why not?

4. In the New Testament, one figure who seems to stand out as friend to others is Barnabas. His name means "son of encouragement" (Acts 4:36) and we constantly find him encouraging others. Read Acts 9:26-28 and Acts 15:36-40. To whom is Barnabas a friend in each text, and how? Who are some people who have encouraged you along the way?

5. "What a friend we have in Jesus" is a familiar hymn. In John's Gospel, Jesus tells the disciples that they are no longer servants, but friends. Spend a few moments in silence, pondering what it means to have Jesus for a friend and what it means to be a friend to Jesus.

Understanding

Every year millions of people make New Year's resolutions, and a large percentage of those resolutions have to do with getting healthier. It makes sense. Countless common illnesses are tied to the things we eat and our failure to stay in shape. We know our own choices are a big part of the reason we don't feel well much of the time.

So it is no surprise that diets and exercise are the top two ways people plan to improve their health. If people only kept their resolutions, we would indeed be a lot healthier—and healthcare costs would plummet. Of course, people don't keep their resolutions. Part of the problem, I suppose, is that diet and exercise involve self-denial, and self-denial is something most of us don't care for much. We think (or at least hope) there must be something that is easier and more fun.

As it turns out, there is. Diet and exercise aren't the only things you can do to improve your health. Making friends is good for your health, too. Research shows that people with friends live longer and healthier lives than those who are isolated. Sociable people get sick less often and recover faster when they do. One study found that those without strong social ties were nearly 20 percent more likely to die within the next ten years, regardless of their current health or occupation. Another study showed that women with friends were less likely to suffer from heart disease, anxiety, or depression. They also registered lower blood pressure and lower rates of diabetes.

Of course, you wouldn't have had to tell the paralyzed man in our text that friends are good for your health. He found out firsthand when his friends made sure he got to see the healer, Jesus. The friends play a key role in this story, as they do in real life. In our culture, heroes are often some version of the Lone Ranger—tough guys who go it alone and usually don't let anyone get too close. But that doesn't actually reflect our lived experiences. In reality, great things usually get accomplished by teams or groups of people who work together. And the folks that make life worth living are those who care about us, our friends.

For the man in need of healing in our story, friends are what make it possible. When his friends see the great crowd, they take the initiative to go up on the roof, remove some of the material, and lower their friend down right in front of Jesus. The man came down through the roof, got Jesus' attention, and was healed. And it only happened because he had friends who lifted him up, and he had friends who let him down. He had friends who had faith that if they could just get their friend in to see Jesus, he could be made well.

In fact, the text acknowledges their faith. It says that Jesus saw *their* faith. For all we know, the paralyzed man might not have had any faith at all. But we know his friends had faith. They believed—perhaps with him, perhaps for him.

We do the same for each other. In our day-to-day lives, believing isn't primarily an individual activity. It is something we normally do together, even with and for each other. We come together to nurture and grow our faith in worship, in Sunday school, in Bible study, in service, and in fellowship. And when we pray for someone, or encourage someone to follow a call they have from God, we are having faith for them and with them.

Faith thrives in community and is sustained by relationships because that is how we were made. In Genesis, when Adam is created, it doesn't take long to see that it is not good for him to be alone. "Not good" in that context refers to normal function. Being alone isn't good for Adam. Alone, he can't do and be all he is meant to do and be. He needs other people. He needs to be in relationships. So do we.

In the earliest centuries of Christianity, the church was often thought of as a boat that carried Christians over the dangerous, chaotic sea toward the kingdom of God. Imagine that boat as one in which there are several sets of oars. On this long journey across the sea, sooner or later, some of those at the oars are going to get tired. Some may despair of ever reaching the kingdom, and give up. When that happens, what should they do? The answer is simple. When you are tired, rest; let someone else take the oars for a while. And if you are despairing, you will be okay as long as you stay in the boat!

If we think of rowing as believing, we see why it is important that everyone believes. But when things happen that make it hard for awhile to believe, it is okay to let others do the believing until we are able again to do it ourselves. When we find ourselves in utter despair, as long as we stay in the boat the faith and faithfulness of others can keep us moving toward the goal.

Because this is the way the church works, it is important that we be there for others. Which others? Jesus told a story to answer that question. Remember the man who came to Jesus and said, "Who is my neighbor?" Jesus answered by telling the story of the good Samaritan. The man was asking which people he was obligated to help. In reply, Jesus told the story of someone who had no obligation to help—who in fact had plenty of reasons *not* to help—and yet helped anyway. Jesus was suggesting that the proper question was not, "To whom *must* I be a neighbor?" but rather, "To whom *may* I be a neighbor?" Who needs me?

Just about everyone needs a friend, especially a spiritual friend—someone who will be there when times are tough, who will lift them up and carry them in prayer, who will listen and not judge, who will keep the faith even when the person in trouble can't. Just about everyone would be better off with another person in his or her life who genuinely cared and was willing to go the extra mile. Who wouldn't want a friend like that?

There is both comfort and calling in this story. There is comfort in knowing that we don't have to go it alone—that when we are worn down, burnt out, or paralyzed by fear, others can help us. There is calling in the knowledge that sometimes we need to step forward and be the friends that others need. All around us there are people who are hurting, fearful, discouraged—people who need to know that people who care are all around them, too.

Take the comfort. Heed the calling.

Discussion and Action

1. In Genesis we are told that it is "not good" for humans to be alone (Gen. 2:18). Talk about some of the negative effects of loneliness and isolation. Include physical, emotional, and spiritual effects.
2. Being alone is not always bad. In fact, just as being alone too much can be harmful, so too can not being alone enough. Discuss the differences between solitude and loneliness or isolation. What turns one into the other?
3. What elements of modern life enhance friendship? What elements of modern life make friendship more difficult or less stable? What, if anything, can be done to enhance or encourage the development of friendships?
4. Shortly after Jesus washes the disciples' feet he says to

them, "I do not call you servants any longer . . . but I have called you friends" (John 15:15). This suggests a shift from a more hierarchical relationship to something more like a partnership. What are the strengths and weaknesses of each type of relationship (hierarchy versus partnership) in an organization? What implications might this have for churches?

5. Many things in life can bring us to our knees, shake our faith, or paralyze our spirits, so many of us have been in a position like that of the man brought by his friends to Jesus. Talk about the people who have "carried you" at times in your life when you needed to be carried. How have you (or could you) express your gratitude?

6. Think of people in your congregation and community who may be struggling to believe in a God of mercy and goodness—people who may be beginning to despair of ever feeling whole again. Brainstorm ways you as individuals or as a group could reach out and lift them up.

7

Out of the Tomb
John 11:1-43

Personal Preparation

1. Read one or more of the following psalms which speak of the sense of being trapped, bound, or in need of deliverance: Psalm 6; 32; 40; 69; 79. Reflect on times in your life when you may have felt this way.
2. Find a copy of the so-called "Serenity Prayer" by Reinhold Niebuhr. It begins, "God, grant me the serenity to accept the things I cannot change . . . ." (Try to find the entire prayer, not the abbreviated version.) Ask yourself what things in your life belong in each category.

Suggestions for Sharing and Prayer

1. As you come together, greet one another and share something that has happened since the last lesson that made you feel more confident or hopeful. If nothing has made you feel more confident or hopeful, share that and ask the group to pray for you.
2. Share memories of times you have felt especially "liberated." What made you feel that way? Did the feeling last? Why, or why not?
3. When Mary and Martha called for Jesus to come help their brother Lazarus, Jesus did not come right away. Use a number scale to rate yourself, with one representing a person who seldom or never puts things off and ten representing a person who puts things off whenever pos-

sible. Share your rating with the group, and give some examples of things you are likely to put off and examples of some things you prefer to do as soon as possible.

4. Review the story of Mary and Martha told in Luke 10:38-42. With which sister do you most identify? How do you feel about how Jesus resolved the matter? If anyone in the group is a "Martha" type, have them share about a time when they stepped out of that role and were more like Mary. What prompted the person to step out of that role? In what way was stepping out of that role liberating?

5. In preparation for prayer, make a list of individuals or groups who may feel trapped, bound, or otherwise in need of deliverance. Remember people nearby and people elsewhere in the world. Consider what form their liberation might take, and what part God's people can play in it. When the list is compiled, have a volunteer read from it. After the name of each individual or group is read, all should respond, "O Lord, set your people free!"

Understanding

When they went to work on August 5, 2010, the workers at the San José gold and copper mine near Copiapó, Chile, simply expected it to be another day of hard, dirty work underground. Had they imagined that they might not see the light of day again for over two months, chances are they never would have gone underground that day. For as we know, while they toiled away, there were two structural failures (collapses) in the main shaft of the mine. Fortunately, the ventilation shafts remained open to provide fresh air.

The trapped miners—thirty-three in all—organized themselves, managed the meager resources they had, and waited. Above ground, a rescue operation quickly got under way. Still, it took sixty-eight days before the first trapped miner, Florencio Ávalos, came to the surface in the special capsule prepared for the operation. As hundreds of millions around the world watched on television, the dramatic rescue of all thirty-three was accomplished. Surely this was a life-changing experience for the men so long trapped and so dramatically rescued. Only time will tell how both the captivity and their liberation will affect them.

In some ways, their experience is similar to that of Lazarus, Jesus' friend, whose liberation from death is described in John 11. In each case, the experience was surely one that challenged and changed those involved. Both the miners and Lazarus had transformative experiences, experiences that had the power to alter how they thought about themselves, about the world, and especially about the future.

Lazarus was the brother of Mary and Martha, who were also friends of Jesus. The story opens with Mary and Martha sending a message to Jesus that their brother is seriously ill. They know Jesus is a healer, and they hope he will come and heal Lazarus. But Jesus doesn't come right away. Instead, he waits a few days. And while he waits, Lazarus dies.

Only after Lazarus has died does Jesus decide to go to Bethany, the village near Jerusalem where Lazarus and his sisters lived. Jesus has already experienced conflict with some of the Jewish authorities from Jerusalem, and he knows that it is risky for him to leave Galilee and go back into Judea. His disciples know it, too, and they try to talk him out of it. But once he has made it clear that he is going, the disciples go along, willing to share the danger.

When they get to Bethany, Jesus talks with Mary and Martha. Then he asks to be taken to the tomb where Lazarus is buried. Once at the tomb, he asks that someone take away the stone. Martha, whom you may remember from the story of Mary and Martha as the more practical, responsible sister, speaks up: "Lord, already there is a stench because he has been dead four days" (11:39). Four days dead without refrigeration or serious embalming results not only in a powerfully unpleasant odor, but also in bloating and decay that isn't pretty.

But Jesus insists. Then, after a prayer—to the surprise of all—Jesus gives a command: "Lazarus, come out!" And out stumbles Lazarus, still wrapped in strips of cloth. To the stunned onlookers, Jesus says, "Unbind him, and let him go."

Other than his own resurrection, this is perhaps the most dramatic miracle in which Jesus is involved. It stunned everyone, and convinced Jesus' enemies that they couldn't wait any longer to take action against him. If word got out, he would become far too popular and there would be no stopping him. The enemies of Jesus even made plans to kill Lazarus, so the evidence of Jesus' power wouldn't be walking around any longer.

The image of Lazarus stumbling forth, still wrapped in bands of cloth, is a powerful and provocative one. It is an image that conveys not only what Jesus can do, but what it may have meant to Lazarus. Take, for example, the fact that Lazarus comes forth still wrapped in bands of cloth. This is reminiscent of Luke's account of Jesus' birth, where the newborn baby is wrapped in bands of cloth. Perhaps the author is trying to tell us that this was a kind of new birth for Lazarus. Jesus' words, "Unbind him, and let him go," make clear that it is a liberation. Jesus' command, "Lazarus, come out!" sends the same message. It is a command that requires a response. It is up to Lazarus to come out and claim his new life.

So it is for us as well. Jesus calls us to come out of tombs, not just on the day of resurrection, but every day. Mary and Martha thought Lazarus would have to wait for the universal day of resurrection to come out of the tomb, but it wasn't so. Jesus was making the point that the promise of resurrection in the future is meant to encourage us to step out of any and all "tombs" we might find ourselves in while we are still living.

Tombs are places of hopelessness. Tombs are situations where it seems nothing good can happen. Tombs are dark places, where people aren't able to dream. Tombs are locations where life stinks and everything decays around us, locations where we are cut off from life and the living, from being the people we are meant to be.

Lots of people find themselves in tombs long before they die. For some, it is a job or a lifestyle in which they feel confined, trapped, in darkness. Sometimes a job is just a way to make a living, and that's okay. But some jobs actually feel like a tomb—a place you go to die a little every day, a place where you are trapped doing things you not only don't like but don't believe in, things that keep you from being *you*.

Jobs aren't the only tombs we can find ourselves trapped in. Sometimes relationships feel like tombs. Abusive relationships especially can feel more like death than life. Financial troubles can also feel like a tomb. Not being able to pay our bills, getting calls from debt collectors, threats of foreclosure—it can make you feel like you have lost control of what is happening in your life. That is part of what it means to be dead—to be powerless. Living in a system of widespread poverty can also feel like living in a tomb.

The story of Lazarus reminds us that Jesus is a liberator and that God does not want us to lose hope when we find ourselves "entombed" by circumstances. It is not God's voice that is whispering, "Abandon hope. It's no use to try. Just accept it." God's voice is the one whispering the opposite. Jesus' voice is the one calling to us as he called to Lazarus, "Come out!"

The power of the resurrection is greater than the powers that want to keep us trapped—the powers that steal hope and destroy life. And when we are the onlookers rather than the ones commanded to come out, then Jesus' voice is the one telling us, "Unbind them, and let them go." We are called to share in God's liberating work.

Discussion and Action

1. Remember that the works of power Jesus performs in John's Gospel are called "signs." Read John 20:30-31. Then discuss what the author of the Gospel saw as the purpose of the signs. What does the particular "sign" of the raising of Lazarus ask us to believe about Jesus?

2. The raising of Lazarus is sometimes referred to as resuscitation rather than a resurrection, since Lazarus was presumably restored simply to natural life and died again at some later time. Nonetheless, the experience surely changed his outlook and perspective. Share how you think Lazarus' outlook and perspective may have changed. If a member of the group has ever emerged from a particularly dire situation or crisis, have them share if it changed their perspective, and if so, how.

3. Note the dialogue between Jesus and Martha in verses 23-26. Martha believes that God's salvation belongs to the future, and that Jesus has come only to invite others to wait faithfully for it to arrive. Jesus counters that he has brought salvation already; he is already one who sets us free. Talk about ways a "someday" or "future only" faith can lead us astray. In what ways may we be settling for less than Jesus wants to accomplish in us and through us?

4. Jesus raised Lazarus, even though it put both him and Lazarus in danger (read John 12:10-11). This remains a world in which doing the right thing can get you in trouble. Name some examples. Discuss how you think people find the courage to do these things in spite of the danger.

5. An interesting detail in the story is that Jesus involves the onlookers in the liberation of Lazarus from death. Jesus brings him back to life, but calls on others to "unbind him, and let him go." What are some ways we can participate in Jesus' liberation work today? How can we "unbind" others and support them in their efforts to live a new life?

8

Attitude of Gratitude
Luke 17:11-19

Personal Preparation

1. Using online resources or a Bible dictionary, learn what you can about the Samaritans and their relationship with the Jews. Make notes so you can share what you learn with the group.

2. Leprosy automatically made one an outsider in the biblical world. Try to imagine what it must have been like for lepers to be excluded and required to warn others of the danger of "contamination."

3. Take the time to make a special expression of gratitude to someone who has been a source of blessing or healing in your life. Call, send an e-mail, write a letter, or speak to them in person.

Suggestions for Sharing and Prayer

1. Gather and greet one another. Then spend a few moments in silence, individually reflecting on the ways in which the world—and even Christianity—is divided into groups that are filled with animosity toward each other. Offer silent prayers for peace and reconciliation.

2. Review the following New Testament texts dealing with Samaritans: Luke 9:51-56; John 4:1-9, 21-24; John 8:48. As a group, attempt to summarize what these texts tell us about Samaritans in the first century and about their relationship to Judaism and Jews. Then add anything

you learned from the research suggested in the personal preparation section.

3. Share times you have had someone act as a good Samaritan toward you. Share a time you have acted as a good Samaritan toward someone else. Discuss what you think makes people willing and able to reach out to strangers in need, especially when those strangers are clearly of another class or culture.

4. The book of Acts (1:8; 8:1; 9:31) suggests that the early church quickly became a community in which Jews and Samaritans could live and worship together. Name some examples of ways in which the church is still succeeding in bringing people of different backgrounds and ethnicities together.

5. In the text that is the basis for this lesson, suffering seems to be the thing that, at least temporarily, bridges the gap between Jews and Samaritans. Discuss how suffering can bring people together or cause them to overlook differences. Of course, suffering does not always have such an effect. Discuss what can happen instead.

6. Share some memorable expressions of gratitude that you have experienced, either as the one expressing thanks, the one receiving thanks, or simply as a bystander. Brainstorm some creative ways to express gratitude to people who have been a blessing. Be sure to go beyond words to actions and offerings. Beyond prayer, what are some of the ways we can thank God?

Understanding

A recent Pew Research Center study showed that most Americans don't know many of the basic facts about the religion they practice. This includes Christians (both Protestants and Roman Catholics), plus Jews and Muslims. For instance, only about half of Americans know that the Golden Rule is *not* one of the Ten Commandments, and less than half could name the four Gospels that start the New Testament. In addition, many people don't realize that a number of common phrases and expressions have come from the Bible—phrases like "a drop in the bucket," "a fly in the ointment," "a thorn in the flesh," "a wolf in sheep's clothing," "by the skin of your teeth," "forbidden fruit," "living off the fat of the land," "no rest for the wicked," "in the twinkling of an eye," "sour grapes," or "the writing is on the wall."

One phrase from scripture that many *do* recognize is the expression, "good Samaritan." It is a popular name for hospitals and other care-giving agencies. There is even a "good Samaritan" law that is designed to protect people who stop to help someone in need. The expression, "good Samaritan," comes from Luke 10, where Jesus answers a question by telling a story about a Samaritan who was willing to help a stranger in need after a priest and a Levite had simply passed by the poor man. Unlike the others, who avoided a fellow human being in distress, the Samaritan came to the man's aid and even provided for his care after taking him to a safe place.

The story of the good Samaritan is rightfully famous and an inspiration to go and do likewise. Nonetheless, the original good Samaritan was only a fictional character in a story Jesus told to teach a lesson, not a real person. Yet a few chapters later in Luke's Gospel, we get to meet an actual living and breathing Samaritan who also turns out to be a pretty good guy. This good Samaritan is one whom Jesus miraculously healed.

The healing takes place in or near a village on the boundary between a Jewish region and a Samaritan region. As you may recall, Jews and Samaritans in general didn't get along too well. The conflict between them went back to the time when the Jews who had been living in captivity in Babylon returned to Jerusalem. The Samaritans were the descendants of Jews who had been left behind and others with whom they had intermarried. There was strong similarity between the two groups, especially when it came to the ritual practices of their respective religions. This similarity, however, did not lead to cooperation or understanding. If anything, it led each to emphasize more strongly the minor differences between them. The relationship between the two groups quickly grew bitter, and remained so for centuries.

By the time Jesus was in ministry, the bitterness was deep on both sides. Ordinarily, Jews and Samaritans went out of their way to avoid each other. But what we find in this village is a special circumstance: Jesus encounters a mixed group. There are ten lepers, at least one of whom is a Samaritan. Despite the long tradition of animosity, this is not so surprising. Leprosy rendered irrelevant the reason Jews usually avoided Samaritans. Jews believed that contact with Samaritans rendered one ritually unclean, or unfit to participate in worship. But since leprosy also made one ritually unclean, a Jew with leprosy wouldn't have to worry about contact with Samaritans.

Furthermore, both Samaritans and Jews required people with leprosy to quarantine themselves. Elsewhere in the New Testament we hear of lepers being required to identify themselves whenever someone was approaching by shouting, "Unclean! Unclean!" It was the responsibility of lepers to prevent others from becoming contaminated. As a result, lepers lived apart from the rest of society. Lepers, isolated from the general population, formed little communities of their own.

This particular community of ten lepers respectfully kept their distance as Jesus approached, but called out in hopes of being healed. Jesus responded by telling them to go and present themselves to the priests. The lepers understood what this meant. It was the job of the priests to certify that a leper had been healed and was thus welcome to worship and to reintegrate into society. Jesus' command meant they had been—or were in the process of being—healed.

So the ten started on their way, doing exactly what Jesus told them to do. But one stopped. This one happened to be a Samaritan. And this Samaritan decided getting certified could wait; something else was more important. There was something else he had to do first—he had to say thank you. It was gratitude that made this Samaritan especially good. His decision to turn back and offer thanks impressed Jesus.

Some who have studied this text have pointed out that all ten lepers were obedient. They did what they were told. Jesus sent them to the priests and they went. The story does not expect us to find fault with the nine. The Samaritan, however, does more than what was commanded. He goes above and beyond by returning to express his gratitude.

This text teaches us something about the power and importance of expressing gratitude. It is certainly a lesson needed in this day and age. Too often people don't feel grateful, even though they're truly blessed. And too often those who do feel grateful let the feeling pass without expressing it. We neglect expressing gratitude even to those closest to us. In fact, many of us are more likely to say thank you to a stranger for a small gesture, like holding a door, than we are to express gratitude to loved ones who really sacrifice to help us or support us.

The importance of gratitude is an important lesson, but it is not the only lesson this text teaches. It has long been recognized that Luke's Gospel offers multiple stories in which people who are ordinarily considered outsiders serve as role models for the insiders. Women, Samaritans, Gentiles, and even tax collectors fulfill this role. The Samaritan healed of leprosy is just one example. By using outsiders as role models, Luke not only conveys lessons about how we should behave, but also challenges the patterns of prejudice and the divisions that existed within the society.

This was important for the early church that first received Luke's Gospel, as it was bringing together people of all kinds of backgrounds into one community. Later on, in the book of Acts, which was written as a companion piece to Luke's Gospel, we see the tension again and again, and we see how the church responds creatively to address it. We see this, for example, in the appointment of deacons in Acts 6 and in the decision of the Jerusalem Council in Acts 15 regarding the mission to the Gentiles.

This second lesson is also important for the church today, as many congregations continue to deal with tensions created when Christians of different backgrounds come together. Luke's Gospel and many other parts of the New Testament warn us to be constantly on our guard against attitudes that exclude or alienate those who are not like us. We are one body in Christ, a fulfillment of the prophet's proclamation that all nations will come together to give glory to God.

Discussion and Action

1. Name some of the divisions in the world and the church today that resemble the division between Jews and Samaritans during Jesus' earthly ministry. Choose two or three and try to list some of the specific areas of contention or disagreement between the groups involved. Share anything you may know about efforts to work toward reconciliation between these groups.

2. Share any experiences you have had in racially or culturally mixed groups or friendships. How did you come to be part of such a group or friendship? How did you address and/or manage the differences?

3. In spite of the prevalent animosity to Samaritans felt by many of his Jewish contemporaries, Jesus seems to relate well to Samaritans and even casts one as a hero in his famous parable of the good Samaritan. This most certainly cost Jesus some popularity and perhaps some followers. Where do you see the church today as willing to take unpopular stands, even at the risk of losing popularity or members? Where would you like to see the church be bolder in taking such a stand?

4. Only one leper returned to thank Jesus. Some argue that the other nine did nothing wrong, since they simply continued to do what Jesus instructed. Do you agree? Why, or why not?

5. Discuss how we learn to be grateful. How do we teach children to be grateful? What are the forces or factors in life that may keep us from expressing gratitude as often and as freely as we should? How does expressing gratitude benefit the one who offers it, and how does it benefit the one who receives it?

6. Close the sharing time by reading John 17:20-23, where Jesus emphasizes the unity he wants to exist among his followers. Spend a few minutes thinking about practical steps you can take to promote unity and increase diversity in your congregation.

9

Calming the Wind and the Waves
Matthew 8:23-27

Personal Preparation

1. Recall memories you have of being on or near large bodies of water. Try to remember the sight, sound, and aroma of the water, and how it made you feel. Imagine yourself on or near water, at peace, with a keen sense of the presence and protection of God. Use this image for a minute or more of meditation each day before or after your prayer time.
2. Read Psalm 107:23-29. Try to imagine the terror of being caught up in the midst of a storm.
3. Look for hymns or songs that use the image of a storm or storms; bring one or more to share with the group.

Suggestions for Sharing and Prayer

1. As you gather, greet each other with the traditional phrase, "Peace be with you," along with the reply, "And also with you." Share with one another one thing that helps you feel peaceful or secure, especially in times of fear or stress. Bring the gathering time to a close with this brief prayer, said in unison: "Lord of the earth, skies, and seas, come be among us. Teach us again to trust you through every storm of life. Amen."
2. As a group, share your memories of some of the watery disasters of recent years, like the tsunami in Indonesia or Hurricane Katrina on the U.S. Gulf Coast. If anyone

in the group has firsthand experience with a major
storm or other natural disaster, invite that person to
share what it was like to go through the experience.

3. "Storms" can be a metaphor for other kinds of experiences that elicit fear and make us feel like we are in a
   dangerous situation that we can't control. Make a list of
   various life experiences people can experience as
   "storms."

4. Share the hymns or songs that you found that use the
   image of a storm or storms. Read some of the lyrics
   together. If no one remembered to bring along a hymn
   or song, read these lyrics of the first stanza of "Stand by
   me" by Charles A. Tindley:

   When the storms of life are raging,
   Stand by me (stand by me);
   When the storms of life are raging,
   Stand by me (stand by me).
   When the world is tossing me,
   Like a ship upon the sea;
   Thou who rulest wind and water,
   Stand by me (stand by me).

Understanding

Nine years ago, my brother and I took my youngest daughter on
a special trip to the Boundary Waters Canoe Area Wilderness in
northern Minnesota. For several days, we traveled through the
wilderness with just a canoe and the supplies we could carry
over the portage trails. Most of the trip was a delight, but there
was one day when we set out across a very large lake against a
considerable headwind. The water was choppy, and we strug-
gled to make progress. It often seemed we were going more
sideways than forward. I began to grow nervous and uncertain
about making it to the other side, but I managed to hide my concern from my daughter. She sat in the middle of the canoe,
clearly relishing the ride.

From time immemorial, large bodies of water have both
frightened and fascinated human beings. People seem to like liv-

ing near oceans, seas, and lakes, but along with the allure there is danger. Storms stir waves, which can make travel on the water hazardous. Hurricanes and earthquakes can cause surges that flood coastal areas, causing hundreds of millions of dollars in damage. Few things are as calming as sitting on the sand listening to the waves roll in, but not every day at the beach is, well, "a day at the beach."

Several episodes in the New Testament take place on or near the Sea of Galilee, also known as Lake Gennesaret, or Lake Tiberias. It is the largest freshwater lake in Israel, roughly thirteen miles long by eight miles wide. Several towns and cities existed on its shores, and fishing was a major industry. As we know, several of the disciples were fishermen.

The calming of the sea is one of the most dramatic of the wonders Jesus worked. It is a story told in all four Gospels. It is one of very few miracles performed without witnesses other than the disciples, and like another (the Transfiguration, see Matt. 17:1-9), it is probably best understood as a kind of *theophany*, or manifestation of God. Old Testament theophanies included God's appearance to Moses in the burning bush and later at Mount Sinai. In calming the sea, Jesus reveals himself to be Immanuel, God with us.

This becomes clear when we dig into what the Old Testament reveals regarding the sea and how the ancient Israelites felt about it. In the Old Testament tradition, the sea was often associated with evil powers. It was a great, uncontrollable force, especially when storms occurred, and a raging sea became a popular metaphor in Hebrew literature for war, invasion, or persecution. The association between evil and the sea went so far that later rabbinic theology imagined both a fiery and a watery hell.

God's power over the chaos and evil associated with the sea is a theme in many psalms. Perhaps one of the most relevant for this study is Psalm 89:8-9:

O Lord God of hosts,
>   who is as mighty as you, O Lord?
>   Your faithfulness surrounds you.
You rule the raging of the sea;
>   when its waves rise, you still them.

In the Old Testament, the power to still the waves is God's alone. Psalm 107 also celebrates this power of God over raging seas. Many scholars believe that verses 23-29 provide the framework for the miracle stories in the New Testament.

The description of how Jesus accomplishes the task of calming the sea is worth noting: he rebukes it. This term is one often used in descriptions of encounters with demons. In the story that follows, the exorcism of the two Gadarenes, the demons are cast out into pigs, which proceed to rush down the steep bank into the sea. The implication is that the demons are returning to their "home," the watery chaos of the sea. Thus, the same evil forces that can take control of persons and cause them to behave erratically and dangerously may also "possess" the water and cause it to become violent. The calming of the sea may be seen, then, as a kind of exorcism.

Yet, while there were many others performing exorcisms on human beings possessed by demons, only God had the power to quiet the sea. When Jesus does so, he prompts awe among his disciples, and a question: "What sort of man is this, that even the winds and the sea obey him?" (Matt. 8:27). The answer was obvious to those familiar with the tradition. This must be, in some way, God among us.

In the early centuries, Christians were well aware of their minority status, their vulnerability, and the periodic outbreaks of persecution that arose like sudden storms. Like the fearful disciples before Jesus awoke, early Christians could be terrified by the very real threats against them; the power threatening them was far beyond their ability to subdue or resist. No wonder the story of Jesus calming the sea was popular among the early Christians. Their visual art and literature often used the boat as a symbol for the church, and portrayed Jesus using his power to calm the troubled seas.

While millions of Christians around the world today face persecution similar to that faced by the early generations of Christians, most of the readers of this lesson do not. Nonetheless, many readers will face situations that evoke similar terror and feelings of powerlessness. For all of us, at one time or another, it seems the world is spinning out of control and we see no way to make it stop. We long for solid ground, but know we are no match for the forces that have us in their grip. It may be illness, a sudden tragedy, loss of a job, or power struggles within a family or congregation that leave us feeling "tossed upon the sea" and helpless.

People may debate whether it is still helpful or reasonable to talk about demons and exorcism, but there is little question that evil is still a factor in our world. By evil, we mean powers against life that are greater than individual actions or intentions. Otherwise "good" people sometimes get caught up in evil. We see this when a crowd turns into a mob, or when people begin to believe that evil means are justified by noble ends—we can lie, cheat, steal, or even kill for a "good" cause.

Jesus certainly thought of evil as a real power that his followers would have to contend with, not only in others but within themselves. Jesus reminded his followers that even when the power seemed too great for them to overcome on their own, God was able to help them. When Jesus taught his disciples to pray, he taught them not only to ask for forgiveness of sins, but also to say, "Deliver us from evil."

The story of Jesus calming the sea, paired with the many stories of exorcism in the Gospels, assure us that Jesus is able to deliver us from evil of all kinds, both that which is outside of us and that which seems to be inside of us. In fact, Jesus as "God among us" may be the only one who can deliver us. Simply remembering this story and its outcome can bring a great calm in times of temptation, turmoil, and chaos.

Discussion and Action

1. Water is obviously necessary for life, and many places in the Bible use positive images of water. For example, find and read Psalm 23:1-2 and Amos 5:24. Still, the Bible often uses water as a negative image. Look at the following texts, and describe how each portrays water as a destructive force: Genesis 7; 2 Samuel 22:16-18; Isaiah 43:1-3; Revelation 21:1-4.

2. Only the disciples witness the act of Jesus calming the storm. For that reason, many see it as primarily a *theophany*, which is an occasion in which God appears to humans in a powerful way. Share times in your lives when God has been made manifest, or seemed especially real or close, to you. What effect did the experience have on your life afterward?

3. The calming of the storm can be seen as a kind of exorcism, or the triumph of God over the forces of evil and chaos. Discuss where there are forces of evil or signs of chaos in the world today, and especially places where some Christians may feel caught like the disciples in the midst of these forces.

4. As the treatment of the text notes, the evil from which Jesus is able to deliver us may exist both within ourselves and outside ourselves. Name some of the ways that forms of "evil" within can create the very "storms" that we fear most. Those who are comfortable may share their own experiences with such "storms" or how friends or loved ones are currently dealing with them.

5. Talk about some of the things other than God that people think can get them through "storms." What are the limits of these other sources of security?

6. By telling and retelling (both in words and in art) the story of Jesus calming the raging sea, early Christians helped one another through many trials and crises. Consider people you know who might need to be reminded of God's power to still the storm, and share ways a person could communicate this good news to someone who needs to hear it.

10

A Fishing Story
Luke 5:1-11

Personal Preparation

1. The metaphor of "fishing for people" is an unusual one,
   seldom used outside the church. Yet we do often speak
   of people being "hooked" by something. That something can be either good or bad. Recall the last time you
   got "hooked" on something positive. Was there a "fish-
   erman" (or woman) involved? If so, what did that person say or do?

2. If you happen to get to a store that sells fishing equip-
   ment, stroll through that section to see the variety of
   baits and lures available. Think about different individuals, churches, and denominations as different kinds of
   bait. Ask yourself what you and your congregation can
   offer to attract others.

Suggestions for Sharing and Prayer

1. As you come together, tell each person you greet how
   big the biggest fish you ever caught was. If you have
   never fished, talk about whether you would like to try it,
   and why or why not.

2. In the New Testament, each of Jesus' disciples is called
   to a kind of career change. Invite those in the group who
   have changed careers share when, how, and why they
   changed, along with how satisfied they are with the

change. Then invite those in the group who have not changed careers to share what kind of work they would most want to pursue if they were not doing what they are currently doing. Finally, have those who have not started careers share what field attracts them and why.

3. Peter, who has been cleaning his nets, is at first reluctant to go back out to fish when Jesus asks him to do so. Share times you have been initially reluctant to do something, but were later glad you did.

4. Check out some other stories about Peter in the Gospels: Matthew 14:22-31; Mark 8:31-33; Luke 9:28-31; John 13:6-9. Based on these texts and others you may be aware of, discuss how you might describe Peter's character or personality. What strengths and weaknesses might he have as a leader? As a "fisher for people"?

5. Peter's feelings of unworthiness figure prominently in the story of his calling. Share stories of times group members felt unworthy of responsibilities or opportunities offered to them. Talk about what might help someone overcome his or her feelings of inadequacy in order to embrace a call to serve.

6. Have a volunteer lead the group in prayer, asking God to help the members of the group to be open to God's call, and inviting God to bless their efforts to fulfill the calling they receive.

Understanding

Almost forty million Americans go fishing each year. That's more than play golf and tennis combined. Maybe you have "wet a line" before, or perhaps told a story about "the one that got away," and you may even consider yourself serious about fishing. But few people in the United States actually fish for a living. It isn't something we associate with a life of celebrity, yet some who fish for a living have become famous thanks to the Discovery Channel's series, *Deadliest Catch*, about the perils of Alaskan king crab fishing. The program portrays the work as demanding, difficult, and dangerous.

Commercial fishing in the New Testament era was probably much the same. Indeed, it may have been even more difficult because there were no engines to provide the power to move boats or retrieve nets. Strong backs and arms did much of the work that is done today by gasoline and gears. Then, as now, commercial fishing was not a glamorous occupation. Those who entered the field generally followed fathers and worked with brothers in the family business.

This is what we find in our text from the Gospel of Luke. Luke expands on the much briefer accounts of the calling of the first disciples we find in Matthew (4:18-22) and Mark (1:16-20). Matthew and Mark simply have Jesus call out to Peter and the others as he is passing by, but in Luke we learn that the invitation actually comes after a more substantial interaction between Jesus and the disciples, especially Peter.

In Luke's account, Jesus is preaching at the shore of Galilee, and feeling pressed upon by the crowd, asks Peter's permission to use his boat. Peter agrees, and Jesus preaches from the boat, sitting only a short distance offshore. When he has finished preaching, Jesus tells Peter to put out into the deep water and let his nets down for a catch.

It is easy to understand why Peter is reluctant to do so. First, he and the others had just been cleaning their nets, an arduous and time-consuming task that would have to be repeated if they went back out to fish. Second, as Peter explained, they had already fished all night—often the best hours for catching fish— and caught nothing. Still, Peter's respect for Jesus is demonstrated by the fact that he is willing to give it a try, in spite of the work it will cause and his doubts about the likelihood of success.

As even the earliest readers of the Gospel would have suspected, Peter and the others are rewarded for obeying Jesus. They put their nets down and come up with a large catch of fish—so many that their nets begin to break and they must call on other fishermen to help them get all they have caught ashore. The total catch is almost more than two boats can handle.

It is easy to overlook the fact that for commercial fishermen, this kind of catch was a sort of financial windfall. Perhaps the most natural response for Peter would have been to begin to celebrate his good fortune. But Peter responds very differently. He doesn't think of what has happened as simply a lucky break; he recognizes a miracle and a miracle worker. He believes that Jesus is a holy person, and is keenly aware that he himself is not. So he says, "Go away from me, Lord, for I am a sinful man!" Peter feels deeply unworthy and perhaps fears judgment should Jesus come to know more about him.

Peter asks Jesus to go away, but Jesus doesn't. Instead, he invites Peter and the others to do something radical: to become his disciples and "fishers of people." The text tells us that Peter and the others agreed, and left behind their nets, meaning their whole livelihood and way of life.

It is clearly a conversion story and one that fits very well within Luke's Gospel. Luke emphasizes that Jesus came to call not the righteous but sinners to repentance. This includes the disciples. Peter and the others make good disciples, and eventually good evangelists, because they do not presume themselves to be righteous or morally superior. As disciples, they know they have a lot to learn about how to be the people God intends them to be. And as evangelists, they speak as persons who have themselves needed to confess their sins and be forgiven. Both as disciples and evangelists they manifest an essential Christian virtue— humility.

Of course, Peter is not perfect and still has a lot to learn, but at least he starts from the right place. He recognizes that his calling does not depend on his merit. He is not called because he is good or because he is better than most. He is called in spite of who he is, in spite of his sinfulness. He is called as he is, and then is transformed by the grace of God and equipped for what he is called to do.

Peter, in this case, is paradigmatic. That is to say, he is a model for followers of Jesus by which we may measure ourselves. This is especially true when it comes to repentance and humility. These must be part of the foundation of our faith if we are to be faithful and effective in the work to which we are called.

The work to which we are called is our mission. That does not mean we are all called to be missionaries in the traditional sense, but it does mean that we are called to have a part in the larger mission of the church. That mission is the same now as it was for Peter: to show and tell the world about the love of God revealed in Jesus Christ, and to call others to join us in the community of the forgiven. We do that best when we do it humbly.

The more successful or popular we become, individually or as congregations, the easier it is to forget our essential unworthiness and begin to think God has chosen us because we are special. The truth is just the opposite—if we are special, it is because God has chosen us, and God has not chosen us simply to bless us; God has chosen us to use us as God continues to work toward the redemption of all creation.

Peter himself, it appears, had to have this lesson taught to him again. In John's account of Jesus' resurrection appearances, the disciples are again fishing and Jesus again enables them to have a successful catch after hours of fruitless toil (John 21:1-8). Once ashore, Peter sits with Jesus and receives forgiveness for his denials. But that is not all he receives. He also receives a renewed calling. Three times Jesus asks, "Peter, do you love me?" Three times Peter affirms that he does. And each time Jesus responds by saying, "Feed my sheep." Jesus calls Peter to embrace his part in the mission of the church. Jesus invites each of us to do the same.

Discussion and Action

1. Compare this account of the calling of the disciples, which is longer but in many ways similar to that of Matthew and Mark, to that found in John 1:29-40. List the similarities and the differences in the two accounts. Invite group members to share which account bears a greater resemblance to how they became followers of Jesus.

2. Jesus does not argue with Peter's self-assessment that he (Peter) is unworthy. In an age that seems to place a lot of emphasis on self-esteem, does this seem odd? Yet it can be argued that Peter's sense of unworthiness could become an asset in the work to which he is called. How so?

3. Jesus speaks of "catching people" in a way that is very different from that of the prophets. Read Jeremiah 16:14-18 and Ezekiel 29:3-5. Talk about how the prophets use similar language in a different context. How might this background have influenced the way the disciples initially understood the work to which they were being called?

4. The expression, "From now on you will be catching people," is usually taken to refer to the work of evangelism. Like fishing, evangelism can be conducted in many different ways. Discuss what ways of inviting others into a relationship with God you consider most appropriate or effective. What role does Jesus' own ways of "catching people" play in your view of the most appropriate methods?

5. Peter was in some ways a slow learner. He had to learn again and again that he was indeed unworthy and that his calling was not based on merit. Share your own struggles with accepting your relationship with God as a gift of grace rather than something you have earned or deserve.

6. We all share in the mission of the church, which is to show and tell the world about the love of God revealed in Jesus Christ. Have each person in the group name what they feel is their role in that mission. Others may respond with affirmation and suggestions for other ways to serve God that the person might consider.

Bibliography

Eve, Eric. *The Healer from Nazareth: Jesus' Miracles in Historical Context*. London: SPCK Publishing, 2009.

John, Jeffrey. *The Meaning in the Miracles*. Grand Rapids: William B. Eerdmans, 2004.

Keck, Leander, ed. *The New Interpreter's Bible: Matthew–Mark* (Volume 8). Nashville: Abingdon Press 1995.

Keck, Leander, ed. *The New Interpreter's Bible: Luke–John* (Volume 9). Nashville: Abingdon Press 1996.

Twelftree, Graham H. *Jesus the Miracle Worker: A Historical and Theological Study*. Downers Grove: IVP Academic, 1999.

Other Covenant Bible Studies

Brethren Press • 1451 Dundee Avenue • Elgin, Illinois 60120
Phone: 800-441-3712 • Fax: 800-667-8188
e-mail: brethrenpress@brethren.org
www.brethrenpress.com